Bridgestone
BOOKS

The Seven Continents

Europe

by Karen Bush Gibson

Consultant:
Mark Healy
Professor of Geography
William Rainey Harper College
Palatine, Illinois

Capstone
press

Mankato, Minnesota

Bridgestone Books are published by Capstone Press,
151 Good Counsel Drive, P.O. Box 669, Mankato, Minnesota 56002.
www.capstonepress.com

Library of Congress Cataloging-in-Publication Data
Gibson, Karen Bush.
    Europe / Karen Bush Gibson.
    p. cm.—(Bridgestone books. The seven continents)
    Summary: "Describes the continent of Europe, including climate, landforms, plants, animals,
countries, people, as well as Europe and the world"—Provided by publisher.
    Includes bibliographical references and index.
    ISBN-13: 978-0-7368-5429-0 (hardcover)
    ISBN-10: 0-7368-5429-0 (hardcover)
    1. Europe. 2. Europe—Geography. I. Title. II. Series: Seven continents (Mankato, Minn.)
D1051.G54 2006
940—dc22
                                           2005017264

Editorial Credits
Becky Viaene, editor; Patrick D. Dentinger, designer; Kim Brown and Tami Collins, map illustrators;
    Wanda Winch, photo researcher; Scott Thoms, photo editor

Photo Credits
Corbis/Michael S. Lewis, 10 (top); Owen Franken, 6 (left, top right); Royalty-Free, cover (foreground);
    Zefa/K. Hackenberg, 10 (bottom)
Corel, 1
Houserstock/Dave G. Houser, 20
image100, 12 (right)
Map Resources, cover (background)
Peter Arnold, Inc., 18; Lydia Martin, 16; Willem van Blijderveen, 6 (bottom right);
    WWWI/Mark Hamblin, 12 (left)

1 2 3 4 5 6 11 10 09 08 07 06

Table of Contents

Continents of the World

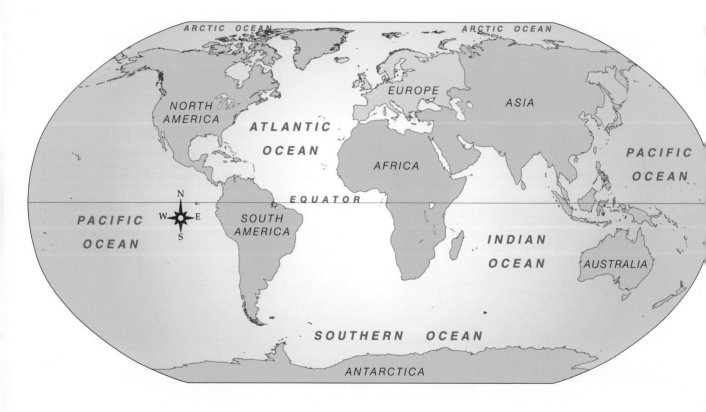

Europe

Each year, millions of people visit Europe. Its art and **architecture** fascinate people worldwide. The many countries and **cultures** of this landmass have influenced people on other continents.

More than 700 million people crowd onto the second smallest of the seven continents. Europe covers about 4 million square miles (10.4 million square kilometers). Despite its small size, this heavily populated continent is an influential part of the world.

◄ The continents of Europe and Asia share land. They are sometimes called Eurasia.

Climate

Warm Atlantic Ocean winds keep most of Europe from getting cold. Temperatures of dry southern European countries rarely drop below freezing. But Europe does have its cold spots. Snow and ice cover parts of Iceland and northern Europe year-round.

Despite having hot, dry weather in the south, Europe is the only continent with no **deserts**. Most of Europe gets more than 20 inches (51 centimeters) of rain each year.

◄ In Europe, warm, wet weather is common. But climates range from the hot, dry south to the cold north.

Landforms of Europe

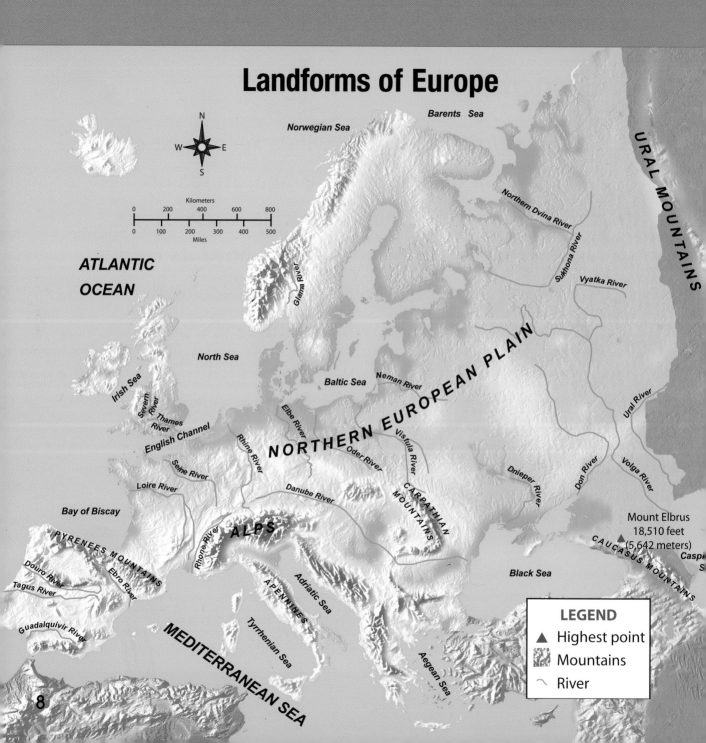

N W E S

Kilometers
0   200   400   600   800
0 100 200 300 400 500
Miles

ATLANTIC OCEAN

Barents Sea

Norwegian Sea

URAL MOUNTAINS

Northern Dvina River

Sukhona River

Vyatka River

North Sea

Baltic Sea

Neman River

NORTHERN EUROPEAN PLAIN

Ural River

Irish Sea

Severn River

Thames River

English Channel

Elbe River

Rhine River

Oder River

Vistula River

Dnieper River

Don River

Volga River

Seine River

Loire River

Danube River

CARPATHIAN MOUNTAINS

Bay of Biscay

PYRENEES MOUNTAINS

Rhone River

ALPS

Mount Elbrus
18,510 feet
(5,642 meters)

CAUCASUS MOUNTAINS

Caspi
S

Douro River

Ebro River

Adriatic Sea

APENNINES

Black Sea

Tagus River

Tyrrhenian Sea

Guadalquivir River

Aegean Sea

MEDITERRANEAN SEA

LEGEND
▲ Highest point
▨ Mountains
⌒ River

8

Landforms

Europeans and tourists ski down Europe's largest mountain range, the Alps. In Russia, hikers climb Europe's highest mountain, Mount Elbrus.

Crops grow on the large, flat Northern European Plain. Farmers use Europe's longest river, the Volga, to water crops.

Europeans depend on oceans and seas. They catch tons of fish from the North Sea and Atlantic Ocean. They also ship goods to Asia on the Mediterranean Sea.

Plants

The types of plants that grow in Europe depend on climate. Farmers grow grains and potatoes in western Europe's warm climate. Olives and grapes grow in hot, dry southern countries. Large forests of evergreen trees grow in cool areas of northern Europe. High in the cold mountains, few plants grow.

Large forests once covered central Europe. Over time, people cut down many trees to build homes. Today, ash, maple, and oak trees have been replanted in central Europe.

◄ Fields of grapes grow in Italy's hot, dry climate.
In Germany, pine trees cover colder northern areas.

Animals

In Europe, people have crowded out many animals. Some large animals, such as reindeer, still make homes in less crowded areas. Today, small animals such as foxes, rabbits, and squirrels, run across Europe's land. Playful Barbary apes climb rocks in Spain. Moles and badgers make tunnels underground. Nightingales sing, while storks catch frogs and fish.

Huge schools of fish swim in the oceans and seas near Europe. Fishermen catch salmon, tuna, and anchovies in these waters.

◄ A hungry red fox searches for rabbits. Barbary apes, the only monkeys left in Europe, look for plants.

Countries of Europe

ARCTIC OCEAN

GREENLAND

Greenland Sea

Kara Sea

Barents Sea

RUSSIA (ASIA)

ICELAND

Norwegian Sea

SWEDEN

FINLAND

NORWAY

Baltic Sea

ESTONIA

LATVIA

RUSSIA

North Sea

DENMARK

LITHUANIA

NETHERLANDS

RUSSIA

BELGIUM

BELARUS

IRELAND

UNITED KINGDOM

POLAND

LUXEMBOURG

GERMANY

CZECH REPUBLIC

UKRAINE

ATLANTIC OCEAN

FRANCE

LIECHTENSTEIN

SLOVAKIA

MOLDOVA

SWITZERLAND

AUSTRIA

HUNGARY

ANDORRA

ROMANIA

Caspian Sea

CROATIA

BOSNIA & HERZEGOVINA

PORTUGAL

MONACO

San Marino

SERBIA & MONTENEGRO

MACEDONIA

Black Sea

SPAIN

SLOVENIA

ITALY

BULGARIA

ASIA

Vatican City

GREECE

EUROPEAN TURKEY

ALBANIA

AFRICA

MALTA

CYPRUS

Mediterranean Sea

14

Countries

Today, 43 countries make up the continent of Europe. Stretching across both Europe and Asia, Russia is the world's largest country. It is almost twice the size of the United States. More than 141 million people live in Russia. Europe's smallest country, Vatican City, covers only 0.17 miles (0.44 kilometers).

Millions of people crowd into European cities. Moscow is Europe's largest city with more than 8.3 million people. London and Berlin both have more than 2 million people.

Population Density of Europe

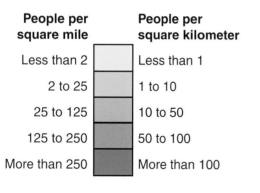

People per square mile		People per square kilometer
Less than 2		Less than 1
2 to 25		1 to 10
25 to 125		10 to 50
125 to 250		50 to 100
More than 250		More than 100

• Major Cities/Urban Centers
More than 7.5 million people

People

Europe is home to more than 700 million people. In most countries, 75 percent of people live in cities. Fewer Europeans live on farms or in the cold northern areas.

More than 50 languages are spoken in Europe. English, French, and German are the most common. Most Europeans speak more than one language.

Christianity has been the main religion in Europe for hundreds of years. Other religions practiced on this continent include Judaism and Islam.

◀ Like these London school children (top), the majority of Europeans live in cities.

Living in Europe

Most Europeans live in houses or apartments. Some wear **traditional** clothes, such as Scottish kilts. Other people wear the latest fashions. France often introduces new clothing trends to the world.

A variety of foods are enjoyed across the continent. Switzerland is known for its cheese and chocolate. People eat sausages with sauerkraut in Germany. In England, people enjoy fried potatoes, called chips, with fish. Italy is known for its pizza and pasta. French bakeries sell pastries and tarts.

◀ People enjoy a meal at an outdoor restaurant in Germany.

Europe and the World

Europe has contributed much to the world. **Democracy**, legal systems, and city **structures** are based on European ideas. European art, science, and education also inspire people worldwide.

Ideas of ancient Greeks and Romans are respected and used by millions. Australia and North and South American countries based much of their government, education, and art on these ideas. Even today, Europeans continue to influence people around the globe.

◀ Built almost 2,000 years ago, in Rome, Italy, the huge Colosseum was a model for structures built worldwide.

Glossary

architecture (AR-ki-tek-chur)—the style in which buildings are designed

crop (KROP)—grain, fruit, or vegetables grown in large amounts that are often used for food

culture (KUHL-chur)—a people's way of life, ideas, art, customs, and traditions

democracy (de-MOK-ruh-see)—a type of government in which people vote for their leaders

desert (DEZ-urt)—a very dry area of land; deserts receive less than 10 inches (25 centimeters) of rain each year.

structure (STRUHK-chur)—the organization of something or the way that it is put together

traditional (truh-DISH-uhn-uhl)—the styles, manners, and ways of the past

Read More

Sayre, April Pulley. *Hello, Europe!* Our Amazing Continents. Brookfield, Conn.: Millbrook Press, 2003.

Striveildi, Cheryl. *Europe.* A Buddy Book. Edina, Minn.: Abdo, 2003.

Internet Sites

FactHound offers a safe, fun way to find Internet sites related to this book. All of the sites on FactHound have been researched by our staff.

Here's how:
1. Visit *www.facthound.com*
2. Type in this special code **0736854290** for age-appropriate sites. Or enter a search word related to this book for a more general search.
3. Click on the **Fetch It** button.

FactHound will fetch the best sites for you!

Index